THE CHERRY LANE
GUITAR
CHORD BOOK

Guitar Chords in Theory and Practice | by Arthur Rotfeld

T0087355

Cherry Lane Music Company
Director of Publications/Project Supervisor: Mark Phillips

ISBN: 978-160378-405-4

Visit our website at www.cherrylaneprint.com

Contents

Introduction

The Cherry Lane Guitar Chord Book presents a comprehensive chord dictionary illustrated with scores of musical examples that demonstrate actual chord usage in various songs and progressions covering a multitude of styles.

The fundamental theory, including all the basics on chord construction, is explained in an introductory section, which also presents charts on how to find, build, and modify chords. The chord dictionary contains sections on open chords, barre chords, jazzy chords, open-tuning chords, and even chords for specific styles. Each section has its own musical examples to show how every chord can actually be used in real world progressions. There are performance notes that discuss fingerings, history, and explain the how and why of each progression.

—Arthur Rotfeld

About the Author

Arthur Rotfeld is a guitarist, composer, teacher, and clinician. He received bachelor degrees in education and jazz studies from the University of Bridgeport and earned a Master of Fine Arts in composition from the Conservatory of Music at SUNY Purchase. Arthur is a private instructor of guitar, bass, and piano and teaches music at New York area colleges. He spent five years as the educational music editor at Cherry Lane Music, where he wrote and edited numerous instructional guitar books. Arthur's work has also appeared in various print and online magazines. He lives in White Plains, NY, and performs regularly in the New York metropolitan area. Visit him on the web at www.rotfeld.com.

Chord Frame Explanation

This book uses chord frames exclusively; there is no tablature or standard notation (notes on a staff). Chord frames are diagrams that represent all you need to know to find and play chords. The critical things to understand are:

1. The orientation of the diagram is as if the guitar is standing in front of you; the lower pitched strings (thick ones) are on the left, and the higher pitched strings (thin ones) are on the right. The frets are represented by horizontal lines.
2. An X means that the string is not to be played.
3. An O means the string is to be played open (unfretted).
4. A black circle represents a left-hand finger.
5. The numbers below the diagram represent the recommended fingers (see hand diagram).
6. Parentheses mean that the note and finger numbers are optional.

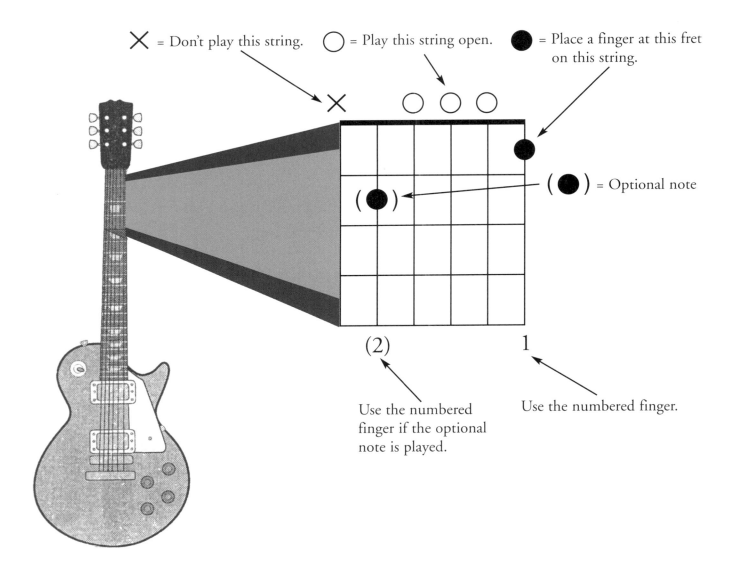

✗ = Don't play this string. ◯ = Play this string open. ● = Place a finger at this fret on this string.

(●) = Optional note

(2) Use the numbered finger if the optional note is played.

1 Use the numbered finger.

Left Hand

Names of the Notes on the Neck

Think of this neck note chart as a chord finder. Each moveable chord in this book is listed in a single location, so it is crucial to know how to move the chord as needed.

Here are the steps to locating a chord on the guitar:

1. Find the diagram of the chord type you need.
2. Determine the root. If it isn't obvious, use this chart to figure out which note is the root. Most of the time the root is present, but not always—a few voicings in the jazzy chords chapter are rootless. In these cases, use the chart to find an important chord tone to use as an organizational reference.
3. Find the new root on your guitar and move the voicing up or down the neck as needed.

Make an effort to understand, and eventually memorize, this chart.

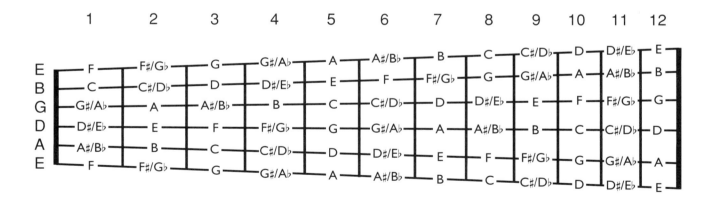

Harmony Fundamentals

Scales and Chord Formulas

Chord construction is often discussed using numbers and formulas. These numbers invariably are tied to degrees of major scales. The notes of a scale are assigned numbers in consecutive order. A sharp (♯) or flat (♭) in a formula tells you that a certain note needs to be raised or lowered, respectively, by a half step. For example, the major chord formula is 1–3–5, which tells us that we need the root (1st), 3rd, and 5th of the major scale to build the chord; the minor chord formula is 1–♭3–5, which tells us we need the root, ♭3rd, and 5th of the major scale to form the chord.

Here is a two-octave C major scale labeled with Arabic numerals:

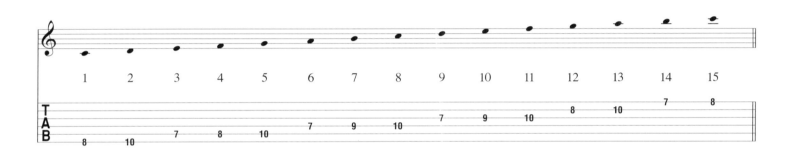

Here is a chart showing the formula for some basic chord types:

Chord	Formula
Major	1-3-5
Minor	1-♭3-5
Diminished	1-♭3-♭5
Augmented	1-3-♯5
Major Seventh	1-3-5-7
Minor Seventh	1-♭3-5-♭7
Dominant Seventh	1-3-5-♭7
Diminished Seventh	1-♭3-♭5-♭♭7
Augmented Seventh	1-3-♯5-♭7

Chord Symbols

Chord symbols are not entirely standardized; the way that they are written varies from musician to musician—and from publisher to publisher. The chart below shows many common chord types and the symbols we'll use, plus the various other ways you might see them (notated in parentheses).

Chord	Symbol	
C major	C	(CM, Cmaj, C△)
C minor	Cm	(Cmi, C−)
C major seven	Cmaj7	(CM7, C△7)
C minor seven	Cm7	(Cmi7, C−7)
C dominant seven	C7	
C diminished seven	C°7	(Cdim7)
C augmented seven	C7♯5	(C7+5, C+7, Caug7)
C minor seven flat five	Cm7♭5	(Cmi7♭5, Cø7)
C seven sharp nine	C7♯9	(C7+9)

Harmonized Scales

Chords are closely related to scales. In fact, nearly all chords can be generated by stacking notes, a 3rd apart, above each scale degree. Studying harmonized scales serves two purposes. First, we can learn what different *chord qualities* sound like (such as major or minor). Second, we can learn what chords built on each *scale degree* sound like (such as what a minor chord sounds like when built on the 2nd degree compared to one built on the 3rd degree).

Here are two versions of a harmonized C major scale:

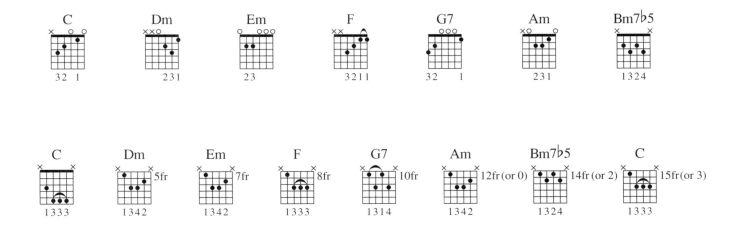

Harmonized Scales in All Keys

Most musicians will eventually memorize the keys and chords found in this chart. Start off by learning the keys you use most often and know what the I, IV, and V chords are. Then, when you are comfortable, add the ii and vi chords. In time, it will be second nature. This knowledge is crucial for understanding how chords function in a progression and essential for transposition (moving progressions to new keys).

I	ii	iii	IV	V	vi	vii
C	Dm	Em	F	G	Am	B°
G	Am	Bm	C	D	Em	F#°
D	Em	F#m	G	A	Bm	C#°
A	Bm	C#m	D	E	F#m	G#°
E	F#m	G#m	A	B	C#m	D#°
B	C#m	D#m	E	F#	G#m	A#°
F#	G#m	A#m	B	C#	D#m	E#°
C#	D#m	E#m	F#	G#	A#m	B#°
F	Gm	Am	B♭	C	Dm	E°
B♭	Cm	Dm	E♭	F	Gm	A°
E♭	Fm	Gm	A♭	B♭	Cm	D°
A♭	B♭m	Cm	D♭	E♭	Fm	G°
D♭	E♭m	Fm	G♭	A♭	B♭m	C°
G♭	A♭m	B♭m	C♭	D♭	E♭m	F°

A Guide to Extension and Alteration

Triads and seventh chords become sonorous jazz harmonies through extensions (adding notes to a chord) and alterations (raising or lowering existing notes or extensions). The basic function of the chord does not change with these devices—every major chord is still a major chord whether it's C, C6 or Cmaj13#11. A general rule is that any major chord-type can be used in place of another, as can any minor for minor, or dominant seventh for dominant seventh. Chord extensions are generated from scales and modes. We know that the formula for a major triad is 1-3-5, so we take those corresponding notes from the major scale. To extend that chord, we simply add on more numbers (notes): 1-3-5-7 for a major seventh chord, 1-3-5-7-9 for a major ninth chord, etc.

Note Function Chart

It's important to know the function of the various notes in a chord, especially if you need to make a change to a chord you already know. For example, if you know C7, but the sheet music says C7#5, it's easy to modify *if* you know which note in your voicing is the 5th. In this case, all you would have to do is move the 5th up a half step.

This chart shows a large section of a guitar neck and relates every possible location to a root (show as **R**). Note that this chart is moveable and not key specific; the lowest displayed fret is not necessarily the 1st fret. Because notes can take on different functions depending on chord type (for example, E♭ is the ♭3rd of Cm7 and also enharmonically the #9 of C7#9) and register (for example, a 2nd is a 9th if it's above the octave) some labels might seem arbitrary. For the purposes of this chart:

$$2 = 9$$
$$♭2 = ♭9$$
$$♭3 = #9$$
$$4 = 11$$
$$#4 = ♭5 = #11$$
$$#5 = ♭6 = ♭13$$
$$13 = 6$$

If you truly master this chart, you might not ever need to look up a chord, as you could devise them entirely on your own!

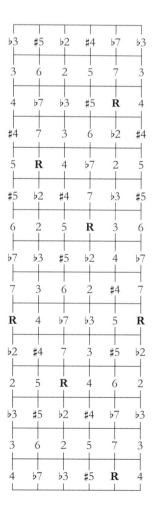

Fingering Chords: Options and General Technique

While some chords demand a certain fingering, for many chords there are several fingering options. It can be hard to say which is best for all occasions and for all players. Let's look at a few different chords and how fingering options can be addressed.

Here are a number of G chords (they all qualify because they contain the notes G, B, and D, though some notes are repeated in different registers). The first two diagrams contain the same exact notes, but notice how different finger numbers are used. You may find that, in certain progressions, one fingering is better than another because it's easier to get to or change from the surrounding chords in the progression. Throughout this book, you may see one fingering presented first, and then when the same chord appears in a different progression, a more convenient fingering may be suggested. You also might notice that one simply "feels better." You have a choice.

The third and fourth G chords are slightly slimmed down. Let the finger on the low E get a bit lazy, and it will lean against and mute the A string for this voicing option. Again, there are two possible fingerings.

The last two chords represent yet another common G chord voicing, again with two fingering options.

And that's just for a simple open-position G chord!

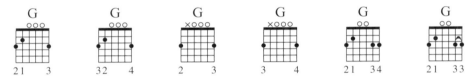

Let's take a look at an A chord. Apart from the first shape, they are all the exact same voicing (spacing of the requisite notes—in this case A, C♯, and E). The first two chords are played with a barre—i.e., using a single finger to fret multiple strings. The very first A chord uses only the middle strings: the barring first finger hyperextends at the distal joint and enables a muting of the high E string. The second A chord would need the finger joint to hyperextend even more so that the middle of the finger rises above the high E, allowing it to ring.

The third, fourth, and fifth A chords represent other fingering options for the exact same chord. It's best to experiment with all of the possibilities to determine which one best suits your fretting hand. Also, be a watchful student and check out how your favorite players and teachers finger the same chords.

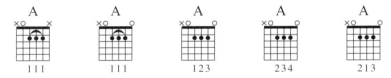

Here's a common voicing of an F♯m7 chord. Two common fingerings are shown first, the second being the most typical, but perhaps harder for beginners. The third example is great for those who are comfortable using the thumb to fret notes. Yes, the thumb is used to play chords in many players' techniques. Although it is frowned upon in classical guitar technique, it appears commonly in styles like rock, jazz, country, or blues. The final chord shows an option for the classical or fingerstylist who can purposely avoid a note inside a barre. A pickstyle approach to this would yield a "wrong note"—in this case the 2nd fret of the A string.

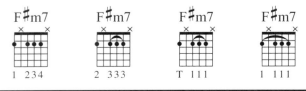

For some chords there are only a few fingering options available. This jazz chord, an F13#9, is impossible to play with a pick unless the thumb is used or the chord is broken up (arpeggiated). The first fingering would require a finger-style approach to avoid sounding the A string. The second fingering involves the thumb, and either the thumb or index finger can graze the A string and mute it sufficiently.

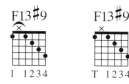

Beginner Chords

Perhaps this is your first guitar book or you are just starting to play the guitar. It would be too assuming to declare that one chord is easier than another or that a certain one is too hard. However, there are general concerns and typically challenging fingerings, so we're presenting some "easy" options here.

This progression uses simple one-finger chords and will get you up and running in no time. Although these shapes appear to be simplistic, they are actually real chords because they contain three different notes. It is very likely that you'll be able to strum these chords in time, with a steady beat, almost right away.

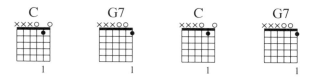

The Am and E chords here are full-fledged chords using five and six strings, respectively. They are great for beginners because the basic finger arrangement and shape is the same for both—just shift from one set of strings to the other and you have a progression.

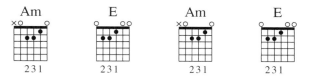

Here's a common set of four chords in the key of G. This progression appears in hundreds of songs. You'll likely find that some chords are easier to get a clear sound from than others. Practice the challenges!

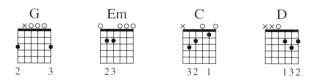

Okay, that D chord was a bit tough, wasn't it? And maybe that C chord was too stretchy for day one. How about trying this progression? It contains a fairly simple movement, despite the fancy-sounding D$^6_9$/F# chord, and it worked for America in their hit "Horse with No Name."

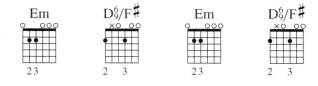

Chapter 1—Open-Position Major and Minor Chords

These are the most common ways to play chords that have open strings or are commonly used in conjunction with such chords.

Major Chords

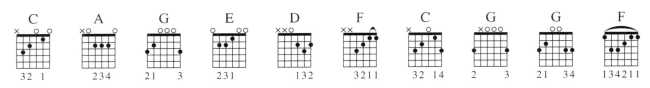

Minor Chords

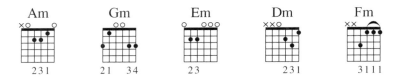

This is a progression in the key of G using all major chords. G is the I, C is the IV, and D is the V.

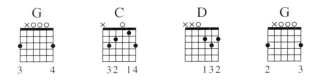

This progression shows another way that the C, D, and G chords might be shuffled. Without any other melodic context, it's hard to say if this is a V–IV–I–V in G or a I–♭VII–IV–I in D.

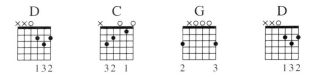

Here's the same progression as the first example, but transposed to a different key. This time A is the I, D is the IV, and E is the V.

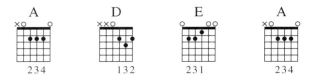

Here's a simple progression that moves back and forth between G and C, the I and IV in G. The Beatles employed these shapes to create a distinctive sound for "Love Me Do."

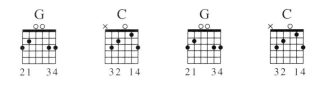

In classical music, the V chord often resolves to the I chord, but in folk and rock styles, it often goes elsewhere. In this progression, used by Neil Young in "Helpless," the V chord (A) goes to the IV (G) before reaching the I (D).

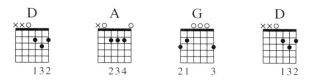

This I–IV–I–V progression is used in the early rock hit "Peggy Sue." The A chord here is fingered using a partial barre, which is a typical technique and one worth mastering.

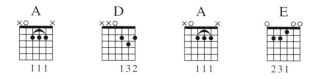

A bluesy character is established by using the G (the ♭III) in between the E (I) and A (IV) in this example.

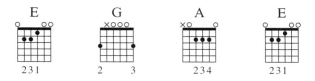

This progression is in A and uses the ♭VII chord (G). Feel free to use the first finger barre for the A chords rather than the fingering suggested, and keep in mind that sounding the open high E string here is not essential.

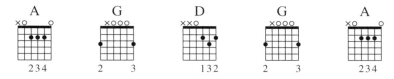

Here's another classic rock-tinged example in the style of Donovan's "Atlantis." It's clearly a I–IV–I–V progression with a D chord sandwiched in. The D is the V/V ("the five of five," meaning the V of the G chord), although it gets interrupted by the IV chord (F).

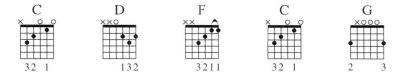

The harmonic minor scale is the backbone for this progression, which is i–iv–i–V–i in A minor. This type of minor scale has a *leading tone*, which is the pitch found a half step below the tonic. The leading tone in this key is G♯ and is a note contained in the E chord (E-G♯-B).

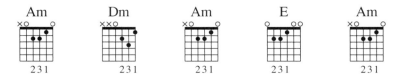

Em and D float back and forth in this gentle modal progression used in the Moody Blues' "Nights in White Satin."

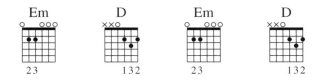

While still in E minor, this part of "Nights in White Satin" uses an F chord, which is the ♭II sound taken from the Phrygian mode (E F G A B C D E).

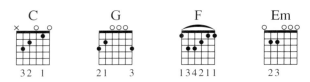

This progression is the very common I–vi–IV–V–I, presented here in G.

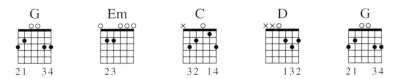

Here's a longer progression in D minor. This progression, which can be analyzed as i–iv–♭VII–♭III–i–V–i, has elements based on the D natural minor scale (the C and F chords) and a taste of the D harmonic minor (the A chord).

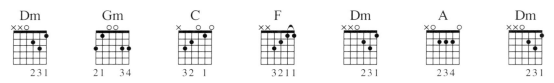

This progression, used in tunes as varied as "Hit the Road, Jack" and "Stray Cat Strut," has a common descending motion from the i (Am) down to the V (E). As in the previous example, there are elements of natural minor (G, the ♭VII) and harmonic minor (E, the V).

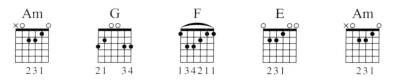

This is the progression used in the Yardbirds' "For Your Love." The key is E minor, but notice the use of two different types of A chords: the A is from E Dorian, and the Am is from E natural minor.

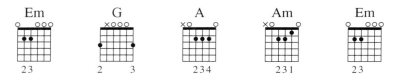

Here's a simple natural minor–based progression in A. By now, you are probably noticing that many chords could change quality (major/minor) to make for subtle, or not so subtle, changes in the sound. Try changing one of these minor chords to major for a whole new look at the progression.

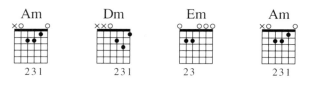

You will probably be familiar with the sound of a major IV chord (F) turning minor (Fm), as it appears in many popular songs. Beginners may find the F chords challenging with the barre shapes (one finger holding down several strings). Be patient and put in daily work—it will happen for you!

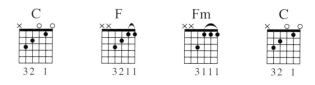

Chapter 2–Open-Position Seventh Chords

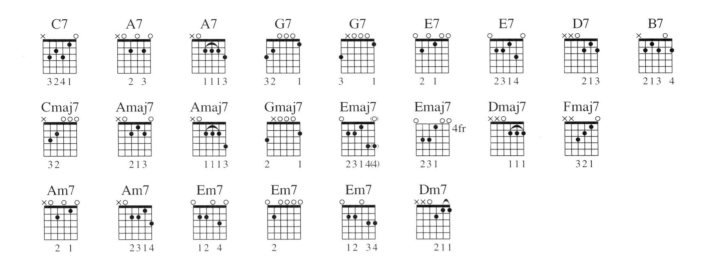

The simple I–IV–V–I progression is back, this time a V7 (D7) chord is used. The V7, or dominant seventh, has a strong pull toward the tonic.

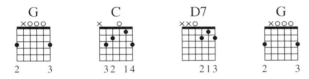

Here's the same progression, but in D. These are the voicings the Beatles used in "Twist and Shout."

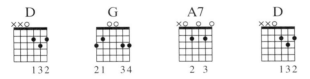

Some styles of music use dominant seventh chords throughout—not just on the V chord. This example shows how sevenths are used in a bluesy progression in A.

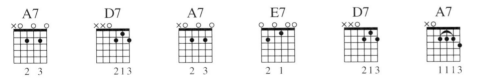

This example demonstrates how seventh chords can be used extensively in a progression. The key here is Em, with E natural minor and E harmonic minor scales generating the harmony.

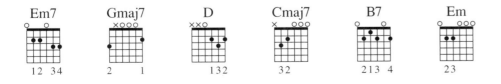

"Knocking on Heaven's Door" has a very simple progression, complete with a pretty Am7 chord, making it a great tune for beginners to learn.

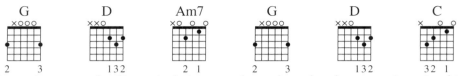

Sometimes a scalar line winds its way through a chord progression. In this example, from Clapton's "Bell Bottom Blues," a chromatic line descends through a few A chord types. The A7 is the V of D. This type of harmony is called a *secondary dominant*—i.e. the dominant of a chord other than the tonic.

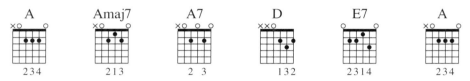

Just for kicks, here's the same progression transposed to the key of D.

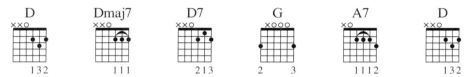

Here's another presentation of the same idea, this time in C and with a twist toward the end.

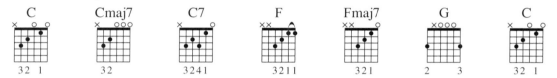

This is another beginner-friendly progression that shows how two different G7 voicings can be used.

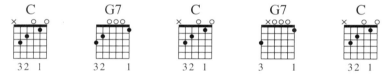

The progression of i to IV is common in a variety of styles. We hear it in more than a few Latin tunes, most notably in "Oye Como Va." Here we can explore this progression with open-position voicings.

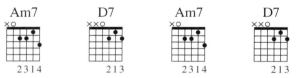

This progression is also a I–IV, but both are major sevenths. The Emaj7 is pretty stretchy, so if you find it too tough, you can substitute an alternate voicing. Another option is to change the fingering. Though a bit unorthodox, some players are able to fret the two notes on fret 2 with the index finger without blocking the first-fret note on the third string.

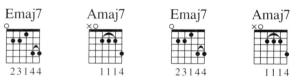

This progression is in D and has a I and IV emphasis, but a taste of the V (A) gives it an added push.

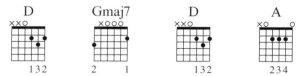

Here's the ubiquitous I–vi–ii–V progression in C played in the open position.

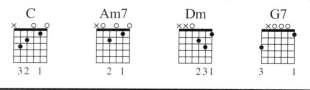

Chapter 3–Open-Position Sus and Add Chords

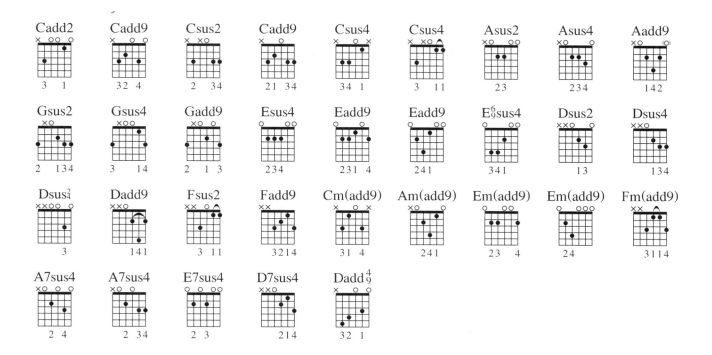

This progression shows how a simple I–vi–IV–V can be enlivened with some sus chords. (A *sus* chord is one that contains a 4th or 2nd in place of the 3rd.) Notice here that the G note is used as a pedal tone above each chord to create a seamless quality between the changes. (A *pedal tone* is a note that is sustained through successive harmonics.)

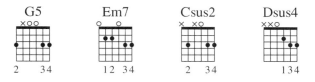

The purpose of this example is to show how a variety of common moves are used on an open D chord. These variations can be executed with a single strum on each chord or with hammer-ons and pull-offs to the suspended notes on the first string for a smoother approach.

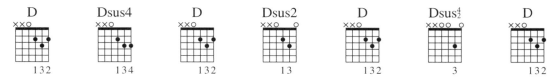

Most of the same sus2 and sus4 melodic movement that we looked at on the D chord can be done on an A chord. Pull-offs and hammer-ons can be a bit more challenging here, so check out the suggested fingerings.

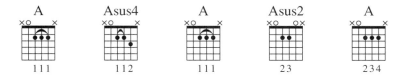

There's not much that's simpler than a I–IV jam in C. To give the progression some color and depth, a 9th is added to the C chord, and a major 7th is added to the F. Instant spice!

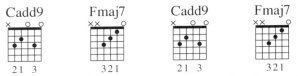

Here's a typical way to use sus4 chords—by resolving them to plain major chords. The first chord is a bit uncommon, but good to know—just be careful to mute the high E string.

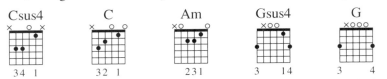

Another example of a high G pedal tone used across several chords, this time it finally resolves to an F♯ note over the D chord.

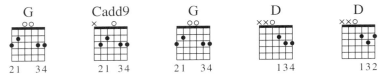

This progression is a I–IV in E and demonstrates the "proper" resolution of sus4 chords. The fingerings of the A chords might need to be adjusted if you can't hyperextend the distal joint to allow the open high E string to ring.

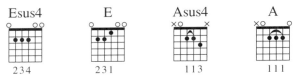

Melodic movement on the D string is used to embellish a C chord in this example. This particular move is not as commonly heard as the moves on the A and D chords.

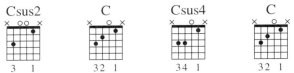

Notice the melodic movement in this pretty progression, ornamented with a variety of add9 chords, all to demonstrate how much can be done to dress up simple C, F, G, and Am chords.

Thinking about the melodic element in chord progressions is always important. In this example, a G pedal tone is held through a I–IV–I in C.

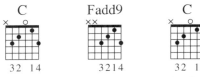

The melodic movement on the high string is particularly strong in this example. Notice how the two C chord voicings are used; switch them and you'll get a whole different melodic character.

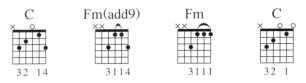

The Cm(add9) shown here is a bit of an usual voicing, but it's not too hard. It's chords like these that get you the good gigs! This progression works with or without the high E string notes.

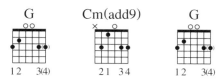

It's stretching time. These chords are not for everyone, so no sweat. Of course, there's nothing wrong with playing only a part of these chords. Try just the upper string parts while a bass player takes the low notes.

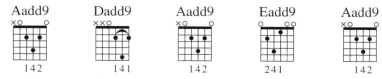

Here's a cycle of dominant seventh chords, each of which is the V of the following chord. The lesson to learn here is how the sus4 chords resolve.

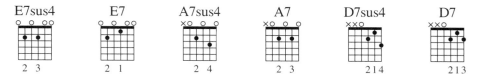

We've learned a few progressions that maintain a single high note over each chord. This progression shows how Oasis does it in their hit "Wonderwall" with two high notes held through each chord. Use a capo on the 2nd fret to match the key of the recording.

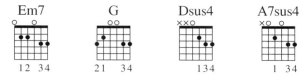

One cool thing to experiment with is sliding open chord shapes up the neck. Every fret will yield a different result—some great sounding, some not so hot. Chapter 8 ("Up-the-Neck Chords with Open Strings") covers this concept in greater detail. Neil Young takes a friendly C chord, bumps it up two frets and gets a type of D chord. This is the basic part of "Sugar Mountain" and has the D chord with an add4 (G) and an add9 (E) yielded by the open strings.

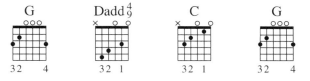

Here's a progression that also makes extensive use of resonating open strings. The second and third chords are essentially F♯m and G♯m shapes, but they get redefined by the surrounding open strings. You might recognize these voicings from the Allman Brothers Band's "Melissa."

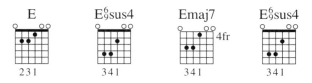

These are some of the chords used in "Dust in the Wind" by Kansas. The intro uses virtually all types of C and Am chords, the interest stemming from the melodic movement on the B string and the Travis-picked fingerstyle pattern.

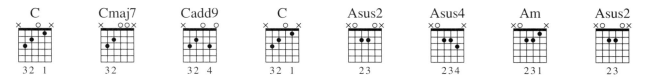

Chapter 4–Open-Position Inversions and Slash Chords

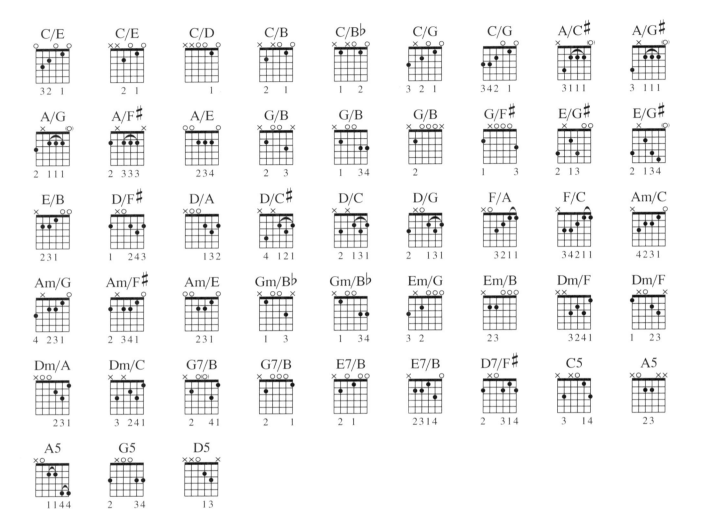

This progression shows how you can integrate chords without 3rds into a progression. A "5" in the chord name signifies that the "chord" contains just a root and 5th.

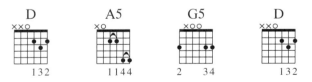

These are the verse chords for Clapton's "Bell Bottom Blues." The notable feature is the descending bass line and, of course, the slash chords. The E/B (read as "E over B") is a regular E fingering, but the low E isn't struck—it's all about the right bass note here, which is a B note, making this an E chord in an inversion (a note other than the root is the bass note). The second Am chord has a G in the bass (lowest note), which is a non-chord tone, so that's a true slash chord rather than an inversion.

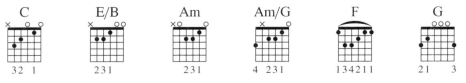

This D minor progression has a descending scalar bass line and includes an inversion of Gm. Try substituting a B♭ chord in place of the Gm/B♭ for a similar sound. You can also look for similar ways to substitute a Gm/B♭ in place of B♭.

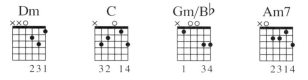

Harmonizing bass lines is a fun musical exercise. This example shows a somewhat chromatic bass line that descends from C down to G with a variety of slash chords—in just one of perhaps dozens of ways to harmonize this line.

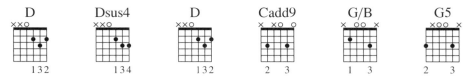

This example shows a descending bass line in D. There is a major IV (G/B) and minor iv (Gm/B♭).

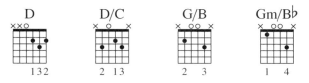

This progression is used in Boston's "More Than a Feeling" and shows a good mix of sus, add, and inverted chords.

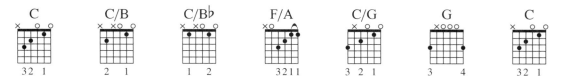

Tom Petty's "Learning to Fly" is a IV–I–vi–V progression in C with some distinctive voicings.

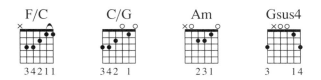

Chapter 5–Power Chords and Major and Minor Barre Chords

Here's a simple progression comprised of various 5th chords ("power chords") that is great for beginners. These are the chords from Tommy Tutone's "867-5309/Jenny."

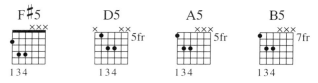

Eric Clapton plays these simple barre shapes when he performs "Cocaine." The trick to these chords is to slightly hyperextend the top joint of the 3rd finger so that it can cover three strings.

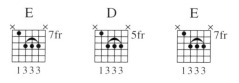

Add one more chord, and you've got all you need to play the intro riff to the Guess Who's "American Woman." This tune, just like "Cocaine," is in E but uses a ♭VII chord.

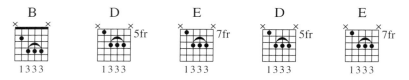

Here's another tune in E that has a ♭VII chord! This time we add an A chord (the IV) to get the Judas Priest classic "Living After Midnight."

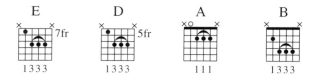

Lenny Kravitz uses mostly full barre chords that cover all six strings for the bulk of this progression used in "Fly Away." As with a lot of rock tunes, it's perfectly fine to use a bunch of major chords built on any scale degree of the major or minor scale.

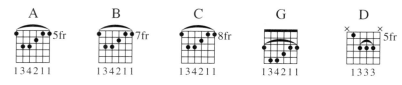

Here are the first few basic chords you can strum for the classic rock staple "Hey Joe."

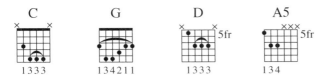

Of course barre chords are great to mix with open-position voicings. This is the i–♭VI–♭VII–i progression used in "Layla."

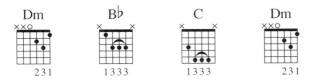

The Everly Brothers use mostly open-position chords in "All I Have to Do Is Dream" but also incorporate barre shapes for the C♯m and B—there's no other way. This song is in E, and the progression is pure major: I–vi–IV–V–I.

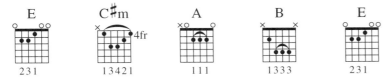

When the Ventures covered the instrumental classic "Walk, Don't Run," they used these barre shapes. Compare this to the open-chord version of the same progression in Chapter 1.

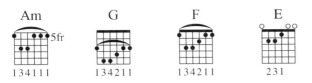

The Cream rocker "White Room" is a great vehicle for working on minor and major shapes on the inside strings. The key is G minor, and the chords are derived from the G harmonized natural minor scale.

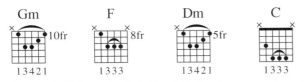

Clapton's "Wonderful Tonight" gives us the chance to work with some leaner voicings that also incorporate inversions.

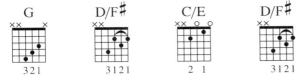

The Bobby Fuller Four classic "I Fought the Law" uses these trimmed-down voicings to great melodic effect. The key is G major, and the chords are I, IV, and V.

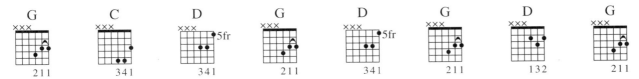

The Cure's "Boys Don't Cry" is a great way to learn the first half of a harmonized major scale. A major is the key, and the chords rise up, I–ii–iii–IV.

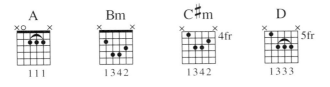

The Jefferson Airplane '60s rock classic "Someone to Love" is a great way to practice the two most common minor chord shapes. This progression is i–iv in F# minor.

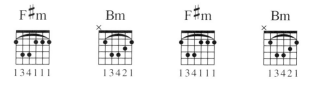

The chorus from "Someone to Love" expands the harmonic palette a bit with the addition of A and E chords. The B chord is the IV in F# minor and comes from the harmonized F# Dorian mode (F# G# A B C# D# E F#).

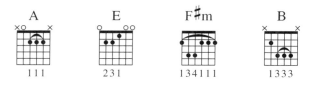

Though Hendrix favored thumb-fingered chords, he used full voicings too, such as these chords used to strum the background pattern in "All Along the Watchtower." The key is C# minor, and the progression uses the i, bVII, and bVI.

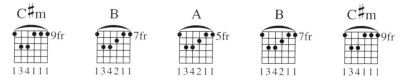

Here's another i–bVII–bVI–V. This particular one is in D minor and is used in the Dire Straits masterpiece "Sultans of Swing."

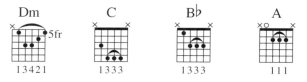

"Sultans of Swing" also features a shift of emphasis to a batch of major chords for a lighter mood. The F, C, and Bb hint at the relative major of F, if only for a moment.

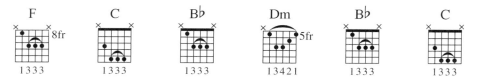

Steppenwolf's "Magic Carpet Ride" uses a V–IV–I progression in G and is a great strumming tune to practice your basic barred major chords.

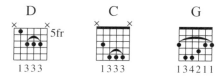

During the breakdown of "Magic Carpet Ride," we get to hear a bluesy progression of I–bIII–IV.

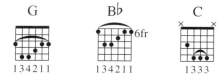

Chapter 6–Seventh and Sus Barre and Moveable Chords

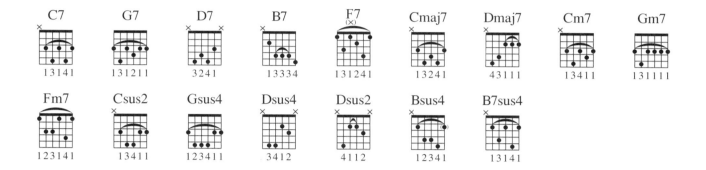

Dominant seventh–type chords are not just for the V chord. In the blues, it's common to also use them on the I and IV chords as well. Here are some seventh chords you can use to play a blues progression in C.

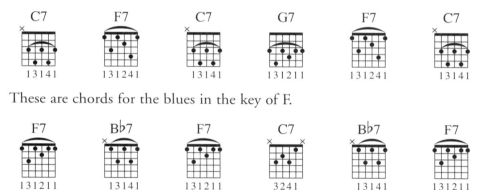

These are chords for the blues in the key of F.

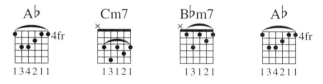

Here's a I–iii–ii–I progression, as heard in the Commodores' "Easy."

Using the major 7th on the IV chord is a common device. Here an example in the key of G.

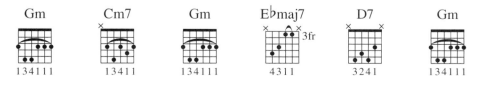

These are the chords you could use in minor blues, such as B.B. King's "The Thrill Is Gone." The i chord in a minor blues is often a plain minor triad, but the other chords are often extended to include 7ths. This progression is in G minor.

Earlier in the book, we learned how to resolve open-position sus chords in typical ways; in this example, we do the same with barre shapes.

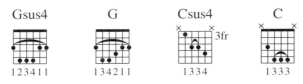

Gsus4   G   Csus4   C

123411   134211   1334   1333

Seventh sus chords can resolve the same way as triad sus chords, with the 4th resolving down to the 3rd.

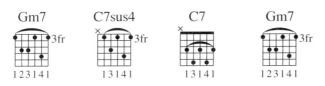

Gm7   C7sus4   C7   Gm7

123141   13141   13141   123141

Let's look at another real-world example. Cream's "Badge" gives us a way to handle a sus2 voicing with the 2nd resolving in the typical upward direction to the 3rd.

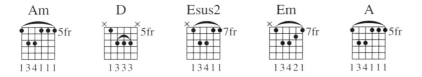

Am   D   Esus2   Em   A

134111   1333   13411   13421   134111

Chapter 7—Moveable Major and Minor Slash Chords

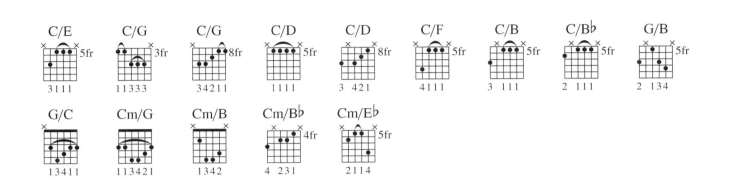

Here's a I–IV–V–I progression like the Troggs' "Wild Thing." The second and third chords are inversions and have the 5th in the bass, which, in this case, contributes to the raucous, garage band sound of this riff.

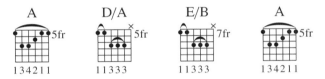

Warren Haynes plays these chords during the verse of his "Soul Shine." It's just a I–V–IV–I, but the voicings are distinctive enough to give it a deeper character.

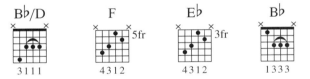

The Band's "The Night They Drove Old Dixie Down" has a unique way of using the I chord with the 5th in the bass (C/G) to create some tension and drama. The sound is unstable, and there is a floating feeling as it goes back and forth with the IV chord (F).

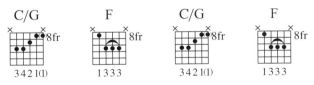

The New Radicals' '90s hit "You Get What You Give" has a simple two-chord progression that uses two slash chords: A/D and G/C. Keep in mind that sometimes these types of chords are just other ways of writing chords that have the same notes. In this case, they could also be called Dmaj9(no3rd) and Cmaj9(no3rd).

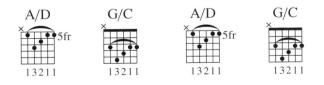

Neil Diamond uses the same type of chord as above in his "You Don't Bring Me Flowers." In this example, the G/C is the result of a pedal tone C running through this part of the progression.

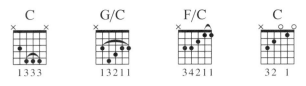

These chords are used in Curtis Mayfield's "People Get Ready," and the G/A has the combination sound of the IV (G) and V (A) at the same time. When played over an A bass, the notes of the G chord sound like the 7th (G), 9th (B), and 11th (D). In that respect, the G/A is really quite like saying A11.

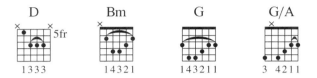

This progression is in G and uses C/D as a dominant seventh–type chord, amounting to a shorthand way of writing D11.

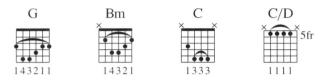

Here's another progression of a harmonized descending bass line. This time, every note from C down to G is used. For the theory minded, the C/B♭ is essentially an inversion of a C7 chord (B♭ is the 7th of a C7 chord) and thus acts as the V of IV (F). The resolution occurs at the F/A that immediately follows.

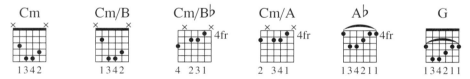

It's common to hear a minor chord with a bass line descending below it as well.

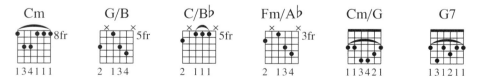

Here's a similar progression, but with more variety in the chords. The other big difference is the lack of an A natural in any of the chords in the progression. Also notice the use of the Cm/G near the end. This is one of the typical classical uses of the i chord in a cadence—with a 5th in the bass.

Chapter 8–Up-the-Neck Chords with Open Strings

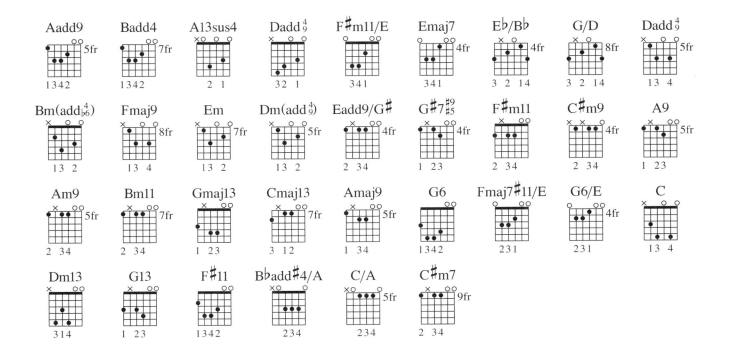

This is another great progression for beginners and is a typical flamenco-type progression. The chords have the basic sound of I, ♭II, and ♭III, all played against a low E note.

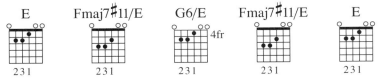

The same flamenco progression is used here, but it's transposed to A. If only a good rasgueado were as easy!

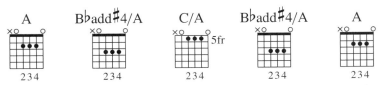

As with many of the chords in this chapter, the basic chord fingering is likely to be familiar. The magic happens from the addition of the open strings. In this example, a simple m7 chord shape drifts up the neck with droning B and high E strings.

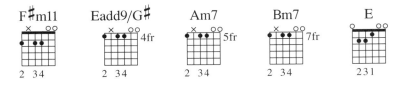

This example involves fretted triads from the C major scale with G and E string drones to provide extensions to the basic harmony. In the case of the C major chord, those notes are already in the chord, so we get some doublings that create an almost 12-string like effect.

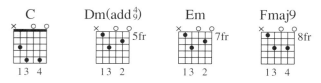

These voicings are common in '70s era Pat Metheny. Again, extensions of the basic harmony come from the open strings.

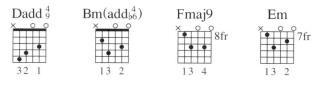

Speaking of the '70s, how about some Yes? "Starship Trooper" makes clever use of the open G string. Steve Howe found the three major chords that include the G note as a chord tone. There's a G in G, of course (G-B-D), a G in E♭ (E♭-G-B♭), and a G in C (C-E-G).

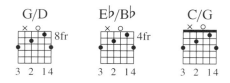

We played this earlier, but in case you missed it, here's the Allman Brothers Band's "Melissa."

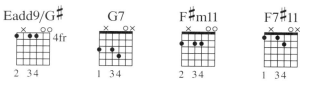

This example is a jazzy way to harmonize a chromatically descending bass line in E.

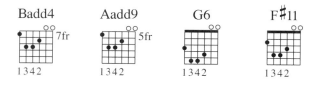

This is yet another way to harmonize the same line, but now there are dominant seventh chords included.

One of the most popular chords to move around the neck is the lowest part of an E-type major barre chord. This example is in B and uses a I–♭VII–♭VI–V progression.

Pat Metheny used these voicings when he played the John Coltrane minor blues "Equinox."

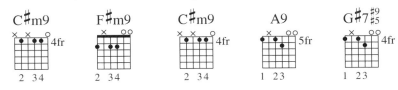

This is a common jazz progression, a I–vi–ii–V, made fresh with upper pedal tones of B and E.

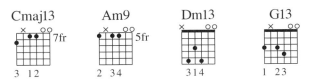

Here's a simple I–ii–iii–ii progression in A.

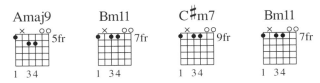

Jimmy Page sometimes used this move, an embellishment to an Am7, in "Gallows Pole."

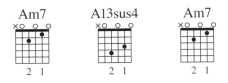

Chapter 9–Moveable Jazzy Chords Based on the Low Strings

Most of the chords in this chapter are "inside" chords (voicings that don't use the first string). These chords are great to use when a full or rich texture is desired.

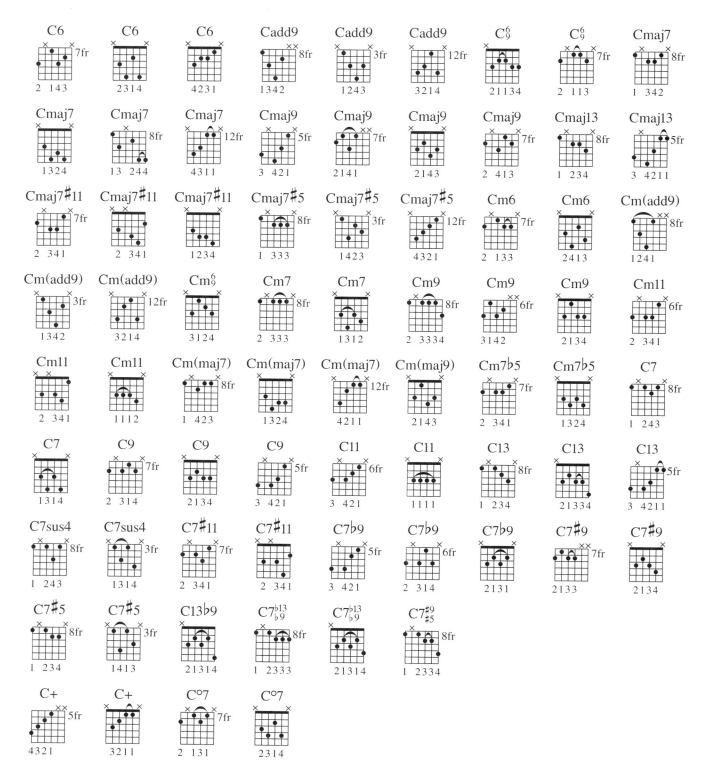

These chords show an old-school jazz approach to the opening chords of the standard "All of Me."

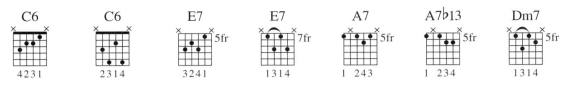

This progression is from the end of the "All of Me" and also uses various sixth chords, which can evoke an early jazz aesthetic.

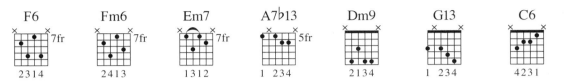

This figure is just an ornamental idea to use in place of a static F chord. You can hear figures like this in endings and in certain tunes, such as Miles Davis's "Seven Steps to Heaven."

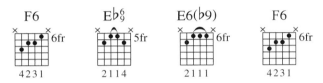

This is a bare bones I–vi–ii–V progression in C. Again, the relatively simple nature of the chords harks back to the swing era.

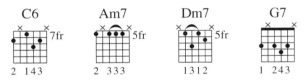

In this I–vi–ii–V, the chords are a bit more extended for color, but are still diatonic to the key and do not have alterations to any notes.

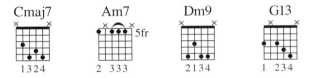

Now we've got a bit more spice and a new key: B♭. Here the I–vi–ii–V idea has an altered VI chord, and the ii chord has become a II (or, more accurately, V/V). This progression qualifies as a bebop-type accompaniment.

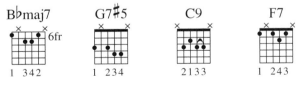

This progression is a cycle of dominant sevenths, just like you'd find in the bridge section of "I Got Rhythm." The idea is that each chord is preceded by its V—the D is V of G, which is V of C, which is V of F.

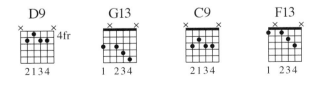

These are the chords from the opening phrase of "There Is No Greater Love." The voice leading is clear here, and you might notice that there are many common tones or otherwise close movements between chords.

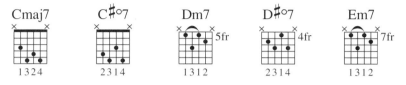

This is the first time we are using a diminished 7th chord in this book. This chord has a ♭3, a ♭5, and a ♭♭7 (which looks and sounds like a 6th; it's just spelled differently). In this progression, the diminished chords serve as a link between various chords from the C major harmonized scale.

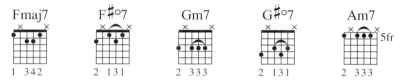

This progression is in F and uses the same types of passing diminished chords as the previous example.

Fmaj7   F#°7   Gm7   G#°7   Am7

This is a fairly hip way to play a ii–V–I. The C♭7♯11 is a *tritone sub*—meaning a dominant seventh a tritone (three whole steps) away from the original is used as a substitution. Much of the time, these chords are interchangeable—here, C♭7♯11 takes the place of F7. If you study them closely, you'll notice that the 3rd and ♭7th of one is the ♭7th and 3rd of the other! Another feature here is the diminished chord used as delayed resolution to the I chord.

Cm11   C♭7♯11   B♭°7   B♭⁶/₉

Here are some voicings for the A section of the bossa nova classic "The Girl from Ipanema."

Fmaj9   G9   Gm9   G♭9   Fmaj9

This progression, from the Sam Rivers composition "Beatrice," uses some modern harmonies and smooth voice leading.

Fsus2   G♭maj7   Fadd9   E♭add9   Dm(add9)   E♭maj9

Though there is a risk of a muddy sound, in the right setting, voicings on the lowest four strings can be very effective; they tend to be underused.

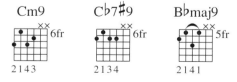

Cm9   C♭7♯9   B♭maj9

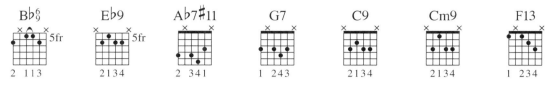

Here's another ii–V–I in B♭. Notice there are two V chords. Many beginning players see a single chord name on a sheet and play one voicing. You are allowed to play more than one voicing per chord and/or to make substitutions!

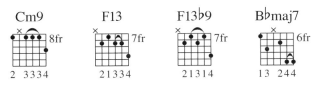

This progression is in F and shows again how a single chord root (in this case, first F, then D) can have multiple voicings built upon it. There is a clear melodic idea weaving on top here. If the thumb-voiced Fmaj9 is not practical for you, feel free to omit the root.

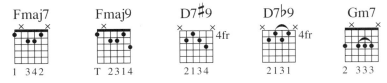

Many tunes have a descending chromatic line inside what is otherwise a single chord. The opening of Ellington's "It Don't Mean a Thing (If It Ain't Got That Swing)" moves a line through a Gm chord yielding Gm, Gm(maj7), Gm7, and Gm6. Again, some thumb-fingered voicings are recommended here.

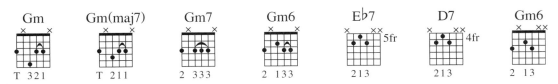

Here's another ii–V–I and for good reason, as these progressions are used extensively in jazz. This example involves a couple of stretchy voicings. Also, here the V chord is shown as ♭II, but that's just a tritone substitution.

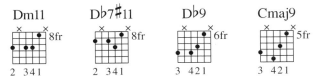

This is the ii–V–I–IV progression found in the perennial standard "Autumn Leaves." The interest here comes from the harmonically extended major chords.

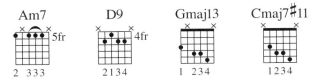

Here's a reharmonization of the same progression. The voicings of the ii–V here sound as if they will lead to a minor key, but surprise! The resolution is to a major chord—and with a raised 5th degree!

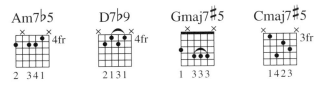

This progression demonstrates how to use sus chords to generate melodic interest in a chord part. There is a recommendation for a thumb fingering here on the C7sus4 chord, but you can also try a 1 2 4 3 fingering, though that's fairly stretchy.

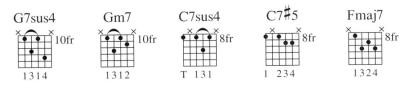

Here's another take on the ii–V–I in F. This time there is some heavily altered action on the V.

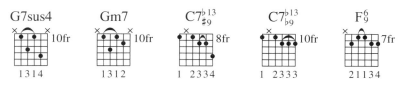

A smooth melodic movement, even on the inside notes, is the goal of this V–I in F minor.

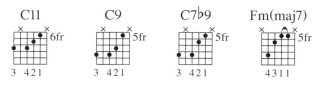

This ii–V–i in F minor has a tritone sub for the V. The G♭9 really sounds like a C7♭5♭13 without a root. A bass player could play G♭ or C under this chord—either works.

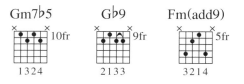

Here's a chromatically descending line played through an Fm tonality. You can use this movement when you have an extended time on a plain F minor. Just let your ear and taste help decide if it works for the particular situation.

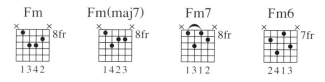

Here's a ii–V–I in B♭ with some common voicings we haven't used much yet.

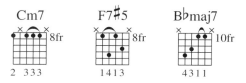

Joe Henderson uses this non-functional progression of chords in the last section of his "Inner Urge" composition. It's a string of paired-up major chords that have root movements a minor 3rd apart, with each pair beginning a whole step lower than the previous. A variety of voicings are used here to generate smooth voice leading.

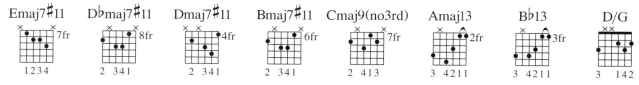

These chords can be used in the first part of Herbie Hancock's classic "Maiden Voyage." Some lead sheets show Am7/D or D9sus4 (and Cm7/F or F9sus4), but the end result is the same batch of notes: D–G–C–E (and F–B♭–E♭–G). Most of the time, eleventh chords omit the 3rd, as it can sound harsh or take away from the effect of the 4th/11th.

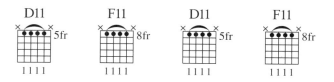

These harmonies are described as types of 11th chords, but upon closer examination, you might notice that they are voicings of various stacked 4th intervals. That's called *quartal harmony*—building chords in 4ths, instead of the very common building in 3rds. This example shows how jazz pianist McCoy Tyner might voice some chords in a D minor modal setting.

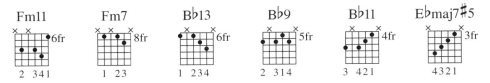

Here's another ii–V–I, but this time the ii and V chords get two voicings each. As mentioned earlier, there's no rule that says just because one chord name appears in the music that you have to stick to only one voicing. In fact, the longer a chord lasts, the more likely a player will vary the voicings. If the last chord is a bit too unsettled for your taste, a simple maj7 could work.

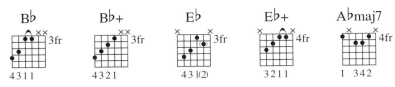

This progression demonstrates how augmented (+) chords can be used to transition from one chord to the next. The ♯5th serves as a chromatic link between the 5th of one chord and the 3rd of the next.

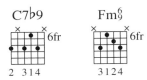

These two chords are great to use for Ellington's "Caravan." Tonic minors are often best as minor chords with added 6ths, 9ths, or maj7ths.

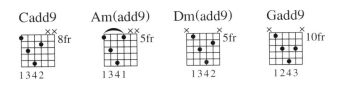

Here's a take on a i–ii–V–i in Dm that uses a colorful Dm(maj9) as the final tonic.

This I–vi–ii–V is made up of all add9 chords and has a fresh, modern sound.

Chapter 10–Moveable Jazzy Chords Based on the High Strings

The chords in this chapter are "outside" chords (voicings that use the top four strings only). These chords work particularly well for chord-melody playing.

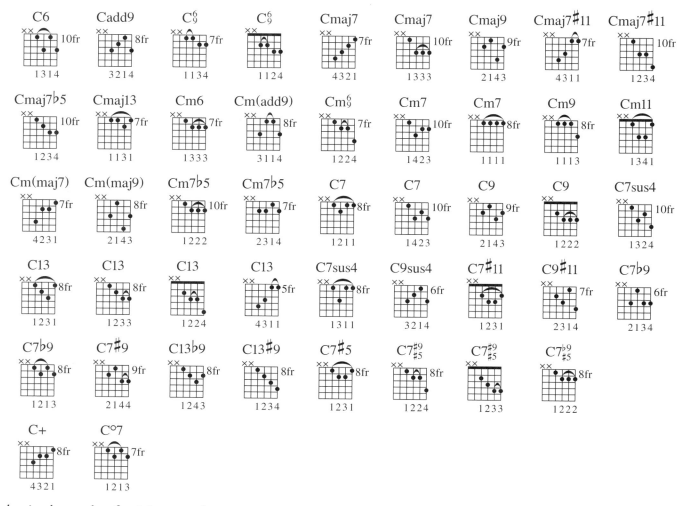

Let's begin the study of voicings on the top strings with a smoothly voiced ii–V–I in B♭. Note that these voicings do not have the root in the bass. These voicings work because they contain all the necessary harmonic information. Additionally, the bass player would likely lay down the root anyway.

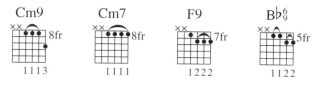

The F13 chord here has no root; only the ♭7th, 9th, 3rd, and 13th are present, but that's plenty to define the harmony.

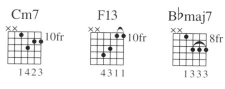

These voicings are perfect to use in the Miles Davis classic "Blue in Green."

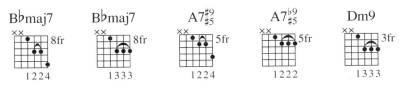

B♭maj7   B♭maj7   A7♯9♯5   A7♭9♯5   Dm9

These are chords you can use in a B♭ blues. Voicings on the upper strings are useful in band situations because they leave plenty of room for the bassist and the soloist.

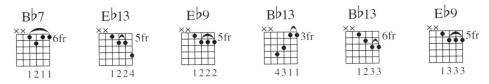

B♭7   E♭13   E♭9   B♭13   B♭13   E♭9

This is a ii–V–i in B♭ minor with a rootless F7♯5♯9 voicing.

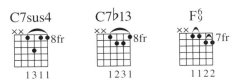

Cm7♭5   F7♯9♯5   B♭m(maj9)

Although this is a V–I progression, the sus chords built on the V imply the ii chord, since the 4th of the V chord is the same note as the ♭7th of the ii chord.

C7sus4   C7♭13   F6/9

This is another take on the same idea, here in F.

C9sus4   C13   Fmaj7

On its own, this D♭7 voicing can be bland, but used as a tritone sub for G7, it comes to life—it's all about setting and usage.

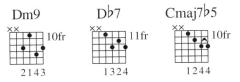

Dm9   D♭7   Cmaj7♭5

We used some passing diminished chords in the last chapter, so here we go again, but with the top strings.

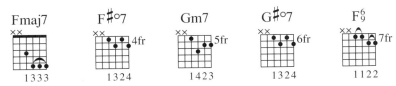

Fmaj7   F♯°7   Gm7   G♯°7   F6/9

This is a ii–V–i in C minor, and we have movement in the tonic area with two distinct voicings.

Dm7♭5   D♭7♭9   Cm(add9)   Cm(maj7)

This ii–V–I is in B♭ and has an almost Western swing sound with its high B♭6 chord.

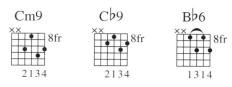

These are more adventurous harmonies for a B♭ blues. The A13#9 is a tritone sub for the expected E♭7 (IV chord).

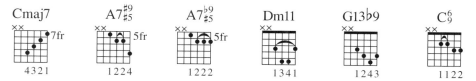

This is a snippet of the standard "Stella by Starlight" and highlights clear voice leading and a sustained B♭ note above each chord.

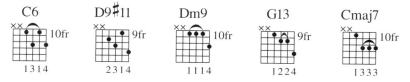

This I–vi–ii–V–I in C gives us the chance to investigate a few new voicings, some of which are rootless. It's valuable to understand how each note functions in a chord, and this becomes even more important with rootless voicings.

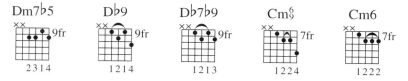

These are chords you can use during the first part of "Take the 'A' Train."

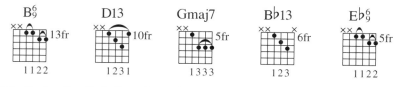

Here's a ii–V–i in C minor. Again we see tritone subs and the use of a m6-based tonic.

Dm7♭5   D♭9   D♭7♭9   Cm⁶/₉   Cm6

The Coltrane tune "Giant Steps" is ideal for working on upper-string voicings. Here is a chord/melody treatment of the opening phrase. Although most of the chords here have four notes, the B♭13 voicing contains only three to accommodate the melody note and maintain the texture.

B⁶/₉   D13   Gmaj7   B♭13   E♭⁶/₉

"Stella by Starlight" ends with some cycling ii–Vs and is a great vehicle for practicing a variety of voicings. Here an effort is made to rise up as the progression implies a descent.

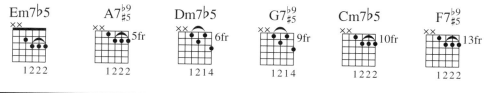

Chapter 11—Open and Altered Tuning Chords

Drop D (DADGBE)

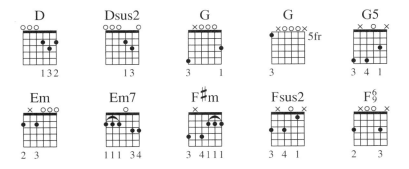

Drop D affords us the luxury of having a really low note below an open D chord, so the sound can be quite different, big, and lush. This example is like what Stephen Stills plays on "Tree Top Flyer."

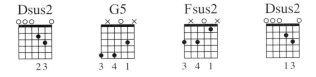

Blind Faith's "Can't Find My Way Home" is another classic that makes the best of Drop D. Of course, the shape of any chords you know on the top five strings remain the same as always, but chords based on a sixth-string root, like F and G, need adjustments to accommodate the lowered sixth string.

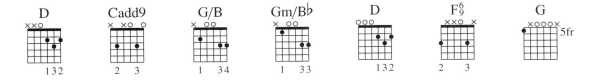

Another excerpt from "Can't Find My Way Home" shows the kinds of modifications needed to finger Em chords and how you might play what used to be full barre chords like F#m.

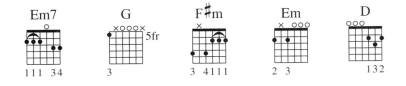

Open G (DGDGBD)

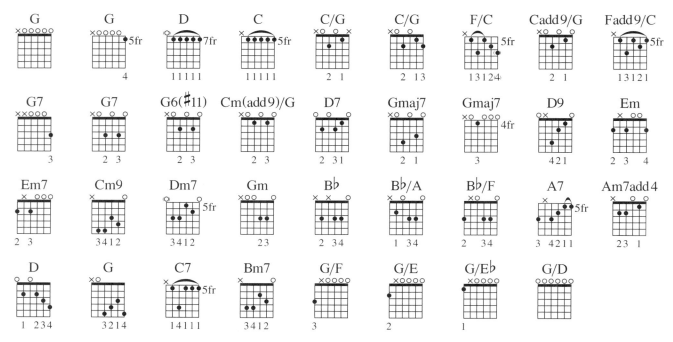

This is how a simple I–vi–IV–V–I progression could be played in open G.

A gutbucket blues riff in G sounds great with these voicings.

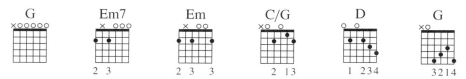

These chords work as the last phrase of a 12-bar blues in G. Notice the interior X in the D7 chord—you'll need to employ a pick-and-fingers technique or otherwise jump over the fifth string.

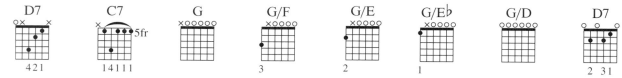

There's no rule that says you have to play in G with open G tuning; in fact, it works great in other keys. Here's a V–IV–I–V/IV progression in D.

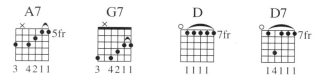

It's hard to play in open G without thinking of one of the tuning's biggest advocates: Keith Richards. These chord voicings figure prominently in his playing. Here are the basic chords for the anthem "Start Me Up." Notice no sixth string is used—Keith actually takes it off his open G guitars.

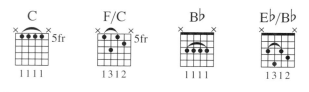

*The **Cherry Lane** Guitar Chord Book*

"Wild Horses" is another Rolling Stones tune that uses open G. Here's a way to play the chords in the opening bars.

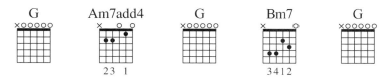

Jimmy Page used plenty of altered and open tunings. He used open G (down a half step) to play "That's the Way" with these simple shapes.

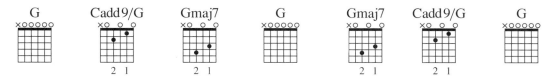

Here's a I–IV–V in G played with one finger. In open G, the low D string can muddy most chords, but feel free to employ it here with the D chord.

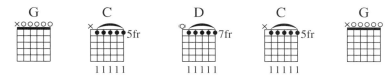

This example shows some of the many possibilities offered by open G and a host of chords, including many B♭ shapes and various minor voicings.

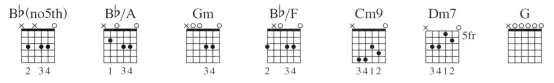

One of the great things about many open tunings is the glorious way blues turnaround figures sound in them.

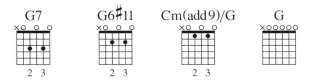

Open D (DADF#AD)

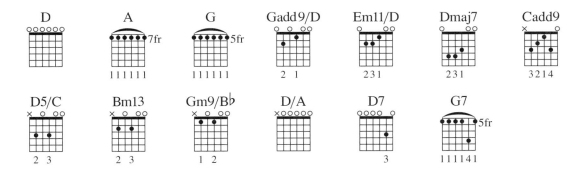

Open D lends itself to simple shapes moving above the open strings

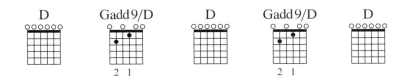

This example is almost the same as the previous one. If you raise all the strings a whole step (open E), you could play "She Talks to Angels" by the Black Crowes.

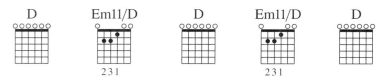

Here's a simple I–IV–V–I in D; the chords are either all open strings or played with single-finger barres—works great for Dolly Parton and her long fingernails!

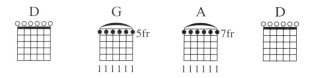

Of course, just because we're tuned to D, doesn't mean we have to play in D. We can play in what's called *cross tuned*. Here's a I–IV–V–I in G, perhaps like Ry Cooder would play.

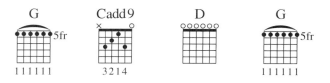

Here's another example in D to demonstrate how some common shapes can be combined with open strings.

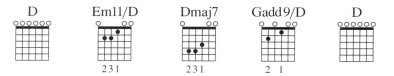

This example shows one of many possibilities for a blues turnaround.

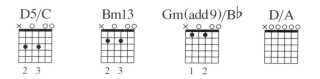

DADGAD

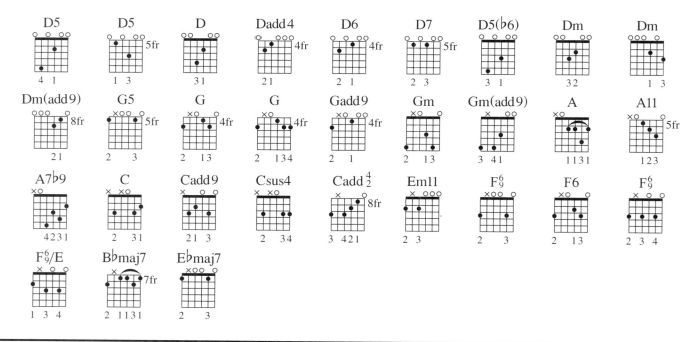

Jimmy Page used DADGAD for a number of compositions, including the Burt Jansch–inspired acoustic classic "Black Mountain Side" and the Led Zeppelin epic "Kashmir."

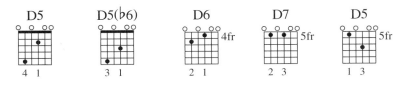

DADGAD is often used in cross tuning, as in this example in the key of G. These voicings make colorful use of open strings.

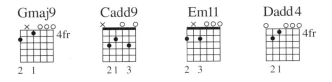

Simple finger shapes can easily be shifted up and down the neck for numerous chords. Since DADGAD has no major or minor bias, it seems even easier to do here.

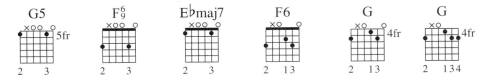

Back in the key of D, here are some I–IV–V–I voicings to try.

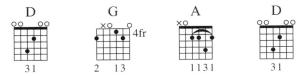

This example is in the key of Dm and shows a number of voicings that are associated with DADGAD king Lawrence Juber.

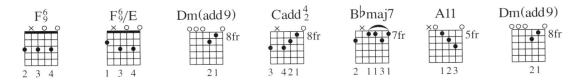

Here's a way to play some Dorian flavored chords in G minor using DADGAD.

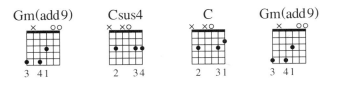

This is a i–iv–V–i in Dm that includes a jazzy altered dominant chord. There's still plenty to discover in DADGAD.

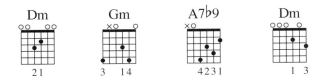

Chapter 12–Chords for Specific Styles

Funk

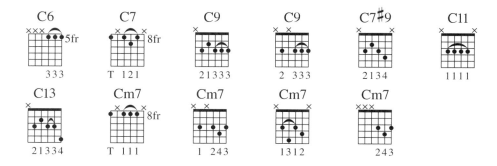

Funk is mostly about rhythmic attitude, and while there are no rules about funk chord voicings, there are certainly some favorites. No self-respecting funky chicken can get by without a trusty 9th chord. If you slide the top part of the voicing up two frets and back down, you'll get a common funk move.

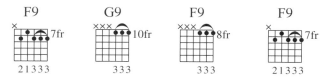

The same shift could be done with a basic m7 chord. Check out this one in F minor.

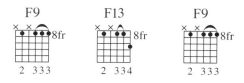

A similar sound can be achieved with the addition of just a single note, as in this one over an F9. The 3rd of the chord is omitted, which is common in the work of James Brown's guitarist Jimmy Nolen or even in Prince's playing.

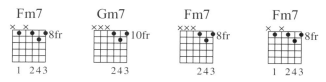

One common funk move is to include a chord directly above or below the main chord. It's usually just for an instant, but it can add a lot of flavor. So, groove on F7♯9 here, but slam out a G♭7♯9 every so often.

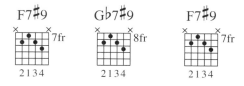

Though many funk tunes use a single chord for a section of an entire song, it's common to use another chord as a sort of entry point. Play the F11 first, but shift immediately to the Fm7—that's the focal point.

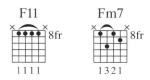

The same thing can be done to achieve a bluesy effect. Don't stay on the Cm7—go straight to the C7.

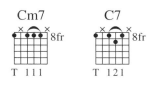

Reggae

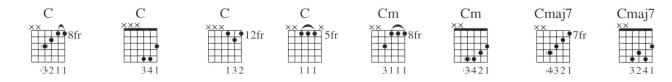

Like funk, reggae is rhythm, but there are some idiomatic chord shapes, such as Bob Marley's small voicings from "Stir It Up."

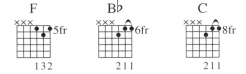

Here's another I–IV–V, this time in F. Learning lots of triads on the upper strings is crucial for learning the reggae style.

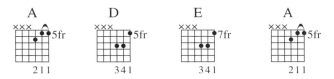

These are the chords for Bob Marley's classic "I Shot the Sheriff." Basic reggae guitar parts contain dry-sounding jabs on beats 2 and 4 called a *skank*.

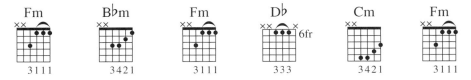

While much of reggae is based on plain triads, other chords work. Marley uses major seventh chords in his "Waiting in Vain." The lowest note is optional, so you can try it with or without. Like classic R&B, reggae grooves are generally established by lean, interlocking parts that involve dialogue between bass, drums, and guitar. The texture is rarely very thick; there's always some breathing room.

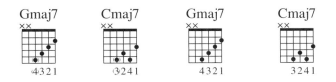

Classic Rock

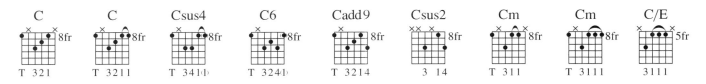

This example, and nearly all that follow, deal with the idiomatic use of thumb-fingered chords in the style of various classic rock guitarists. Here we have the basic progression for "Pinball Wizard." Finger the sixth string with the thumb. It doesn't have to be the tip either; any part that gets the job done is fine. Generally, the area around the joint makes the actual contact.

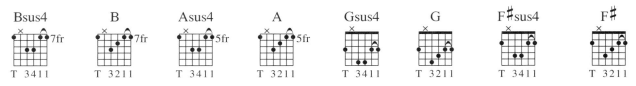

Here's an example that shows a bit of Hendrix's approach in "Purple Haze." The thumb not only frets the low note, but actually mutes the A string. Notice the arrow in the last example—this shows how Hendrix would play this note and then pull off to the lower note.

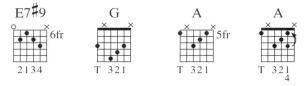

This is the intro to "The Wind Cries Mary." Hendrix begins with some 5th-in-the-bass chords and then goes into some 3rd-in-the-bass chords. Again, the lower notes are immediately "crushed" into the higher notes.

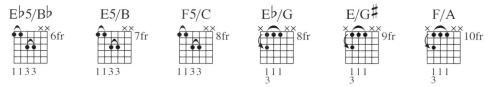

Though not a thumb chord, these Hendrix-style chords are also worth noting. You can leap around with these sus2 shapes to play melodic ideas, as in the intro from "Castles Made of Sand."

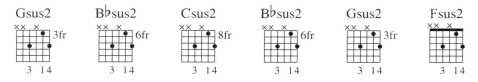

The final example is a i–♭VII–♭VI–♭VII in A minor. The chord voicings are similar to what Jimmy Page often used live in "Stairway to Heaven" right after the guitar solo. In addition to using the thumb to fret the notes, it also mutes the fifth string.

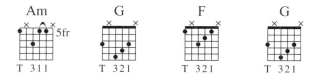